Dear secondary umbilical,

by j/j hastain

*A Prize-Winning Manuscript in the
2012 MadHat Press Wild and Wyrd Poetry Chapbook Competition*

MadHat Press
Asheville, North Carolina

MadHat Press
MadHat Incorporated
PO Box 8364, Asheville, NC 28814

Copyright © 2012-2013 j/j hastain
All rights reserved

ISBN 978-0-9885490-2-9 (paperback)

Text and interior art by j/j hastain
Cover art by Michael Crowley
Book and cover design by MadHat Press and Jonathan Penton

www.madhat-press.com

First Printing

Dear secondary umbilical,

j/j hastain

I consider my work expressive anti-memoir: an entirely new type of book—

Book as place and pace—book as neoteric lace—book as a necessarily transgressive system, invented to shape and share the stories about what can emerge from heightened attention to alchemical instances of crossing—book as a modern Rumi scribing and etching what is comprised of where gender, eros, contemplation, superimposition, reaching, juxtapositions of image, feeling and impulse all interweave to make new worlds and/ or new sensations.

I believe in creating texts/ spaces that are inherently non-linear and a-historical—texts as spaces that have not been patriarchally controlled and cannot be patriarchally controlled. It is my hope that in these spaces there will be room to experience new types of truth, mood, impression, imagination and equity.

Dear secondary umbilical,

"I am not talking about the Justice of the courts but about the other Justice, which is consummated slowly and equally painfully, in the teachings of the great magistrates of mankind, in the political struggles for social liberation and in the loftiest poetic accomplishments. From such a great effort the drops of light fall slowly every now and then into the vast night of the soul like lemon drops into polluted water."

—**What I Love** *Odysseas Elytis*

If the infant's first experiences of unconditional light occur while it is in the womb (even if those experiences are not that of direct light and are instead the **feeling-texture of lattice light** through connection to the host body), the fact that the umbilical cord is severed without the infant's consent is one of the first impositions of violence onto the body.

Dear secondary umbilical, is my vulnerability-record just like the umbilical cord is the infant's vulnerability-record—but in the inverse. The infant's cord gets cut. I am making connections to unconditional light again by way of creating contacts, which are re-adhesions of any first cut.

Dear secondary umbilical,

This is the desire to be bound to. This is the desire to be bound by.

Succulent cravings which are making themselves more and more apparent through ink—through elliptical gesturing.

I begin these letters with awareness that I need a conglomerate body to send all of the disparate parts to.

I admit that I must be stored in a complex, mysterious thing that is living.

Therefore, I am concocting this conglomerate body of luminosities in order to be able to continually contact—in order to touch source-light. I am dreaming each position into a fruition, so that I can lean on ripenesses and into ulterior-edens as the sporadic revelations, contextualizations and poultices emerge.

I wish this conglomerate body as I wish a tome incapable of passing judgment on me.

I wish an unconditional sequence of gods—always verifying and validating so much awash.

j/j hastain

Dear secondary umbilical,

There are always other ways to have begun—methods to pulling at the luscious threads that are hungry for stringcourse, that are ravenous for more—this in order to provide additional merger.

Animate edgery that will hold me as I hold the evolutions in order to ensure more immanence.

I know that together this conglomerate body and I can become a zone of the unconditional offer of calori[1]. Constantly lyrical and elegiac as it intensifies via heat.

This is how I plan to cultivate canticle—as a multiple-paean[2] in attempt at sustaining authentic alternates to any polarist or patriarchal deity. This is the choice to turn what once lived in me as an inviolable, non-solvable sorrow into unbound sentiment.

Spinning the warmed decaying birds into fragrant and consistent after-names, where anathema can become anthem.

---

1   Prefix relating to heat
2   Song of joy and praise

Dear secondary umbilical,

A slowly opening camber for the zygote that is also the antiquity.

If I make documents that are truly beautiful, is that enough to have mattered to the earth?

To have mattered to the ether as earth?

Or is it necessary that I find ways to be held here in a human body—fixed to the earth?

I am interested in feeling the separation between myself in form and myself transcendent of form, as an intricate and purposeful heaviness, rather than as psychosis.

I wonder if I am inherently a shape which exists due to merges and cosmic fusions, rather than due to shapes related to a void?

What would it take in order for me to be an everlasting prodigy of my own multi-planar potential?

I feel that I must be potently admixed, in order to never be impotent or without fecundation.

Dear secondary umbilical,

I find that the more abysmal the love making gets, the more these huge boulders feel like they are being extracted from my esophagus—something like collaborated psychic surgery where nano-ducts and nerve-synonyms are enabled to return to their former states of flexibility.

I am saying that the erotic release through guaranteed orgasm is like the power of superimposed seasons—or a neoteric fuel extracted from thousands of pounds of slowly compressed feathers.

The relief in this coiling and copious oil.

Sonorous and cavernous as we refuse to ever conclude curvature.

> How it is that I actually get my physicality?

My body as a human body identifying with materialities such as: breath, dinner, gentle communication, the warm shower, etc.—each of these are curious vitalities that I am able to feel in the physical, only after you have scored me at the edges of pleasure and sensation—only after we have touched the astral body through sex.

I know that this has to do with non-linear trust—with how the durations of our fucking make it possible, that when I look into the large mirror above our winding stairs I finally notice myself as familiar to myself—as a cosmically authentic identity recalling.

Dear secondary umbilical,

Here where our sensual and sexual movements are co-chant coherences—are unconditionally variegated—are spatial but are never partial.

The wormhole and the womb stay lubricated this way, in solidarities to one another while they become unified. And it is here that I recall bountiful and potency as my birthright.

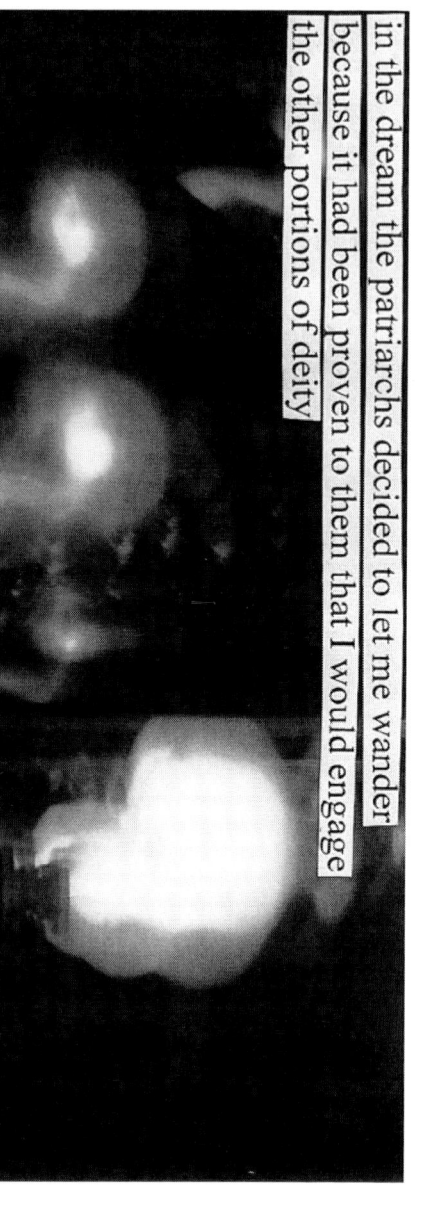

in the dream the patriarchs decided to let me wander because it had been proven to them that I would engage the other portions of deity as I leapt from the edge and plunged into piles and piles of portioned worms they peristalted as a singularity and the image of my understanding was a rounded one as they sucked me further and further into their mass

Dear secondary umbilical,

I am overwhelmed by the feeling that it is my responsibility to mature and evolve as form, no matter what the circumstances of my given contexts are.

Called to be a place of personal upholding for the sake of the importance of homeland—of the aggregate—of eventual.

Urges and urgencies are being refined. Meta-stories are gaining their environments.

The morning when I walked out of my small apartment and the countless worms lay in peristalsis, struggling on the walkway. How I slowly bent down and moved each one of them one at a time, to the saturated grass while humming. Humming more like inverted glow, than like sound.

Noting the significance of the rain on that morning—how it too was a pounding that made stillness within.

This is a discipleship of leavening, showing how the beautiful is reason enough to create tongue for the beautiful.

Similar to the need to know my own un-ownable mouth as an entity that is climaxing in place of it ever being compliant.

To be an unendingly gesticulating image—an effervescing apogee.

Dear secondary umbilical,

I identify as a curious calori-eve, always both wet and incubating through enclave.

> Is a not yet complete heart a partialed orb?
>
> Are these types of shapes cosmically meant to be rectified?
>
> Is the only correctness in the context of not yet completed shapes, to add to them?

When the coffer is re-animated I experience an automatic draw to materialize divergent deities that I know can hold—sempiternals that I can hold as the stunning morphologies continue to take place.

This is the activism of creating alternates to previous _____ so that I can worship perpetually, consistently and concurrently.

Dear secondary umbilical,

Sometimes it is difficult to translate what I learn in the cave if I am my cave.

That there is no external to this work: corollaries, coronaries, perforations, spasms, globules, synonyms, shorelines.

It is here that a lyrical tongue is being applied to a fiercely erotic heart.

It is here that the ingredients make quantum bread.

It is through inward retinas compelling and compiling, enforcing—that lullaby and torque can exist in relation to one another.

Tongue gains its autonomies and identities as a maturing entity once it leaves its lives of non-itinerancy and non-identity behind. From here it materializes—bending the planet until it bleeds new types of breeding.

The fossas and fissures are becoming quixotic—gaining fur.

a cave is a shelter that aches

Dear secondary umbilical,

My ribs are still burning from inside of them. My genitals are still raw and quivering. I am trying to emphasize the importance of reversals of impotence—the reversals which are also guerilla revolutions.

Like chordal diligences—like burlesquing. When we fuck a prayer chamber with the identity and velocity of a tornado appears.

This is the body's deifying need to propagate and feast. This is about sites of attention—about what exceeds the usual—about moments that transcend normalcy or status-quo.

Cock hanging between the legs of a gorgon.

The incredibly large quivering vulva poised as the lips of an opening flower in the Amazon.

These are the ulterior gods spilling their roils.

This is the dangling theatre.

j/j hastain

Dear secondary umbilical,

When I went back into the cave to extract the female spider, I couldn't find her. Instead I found a male spider that I had never seen there before. This experience was like once inconspicuous genitalia in a scene, becoming prominent when it was most needed for inter-ether reference.

I am telling you that I need this. Not sure how else to classify it except to refuse categorization, and to instead describe.

Like what extraterrestrial liquid might mean for the futures.

Like cultivating lucid in order to replace trauma or lacerations.

Like firm, sonorous, contractions.

Dear secondary umbilical,

Take me into a standard of unconditional plethora.

I am asking for this from materiality. I am asking for this from refuted linearity.

I finally identify as effeminate in my body and I want, with a vigilance incomparable to strictly single-planar sentiments.

I want. I want to be fucked—rocked into eternity as eternity.

I want tabernacles, stained glass and hybrid fruit left as the roughage of each engagement.

I want from the inside through force unmitigated by doubt, limit or refusal.

I want it always burgeoning the new, as it burgeons.

Only through this co-activism are the boulders ever removed from my esophagus—only through this is my breath and speech ever more enabled.

This which is like paint slowly being electrocuted.

And sap that is spilling from the aurora borealis which is becoming unkempt between the legs—a place for the inter to drink.

Through these proclamations I am always erecting a next—a next lifetime through this lifetime—to provoke myself via accelerant-phoenixes.

To be resurrected within this shaking site, without ever having to experience deaths based in finality due to_____.

Dear secondary umbilical,

Turritopsis nutricula is a type of jelly fish that reverts to the polyp stage after progressing through sexual maturity. It accomplishes this through a non-typical cell development called transdifferentiation. This process can replicate itself with infinite capacity rendering the jellyfish organically immortal.

Oh immortal jellyfish, both in the context of the dream and the becoming—how something in this has to do with the constantly regenerative virginity. The lumen-hymen. There are many ways that this ever re-combinatory hymen can be applied to future maturations. There is responsibility to this—meaning, making another hymen in order for it to be broken for and through ones purposes and evolutions.

There need be no finality-death in order to live a next life. Finding it is possible to be resurrected without having to pass through any ending. This never to avoid the death per say, but to not have to use any of ones animate time on the death, where it could instead be used in the active morphology of the next organic and infused form, now.

I am saying that our relation does this for me.

Co-devotion—orgiastic adulation of the supple and the secreting. Applying and then conjuring the many supplementary holy places.

Not just the sexual maturity which comes with access and intensity of experience, but the then eternal maturity that comes from truly embodying those maturations in the same ways that a being that does so, recites, intones and counts through their mala beads.

Because sound is a cosmic truth—thereby never the muted pussy.

Dear secondary umbilical,

Perhaps if you passionately love your gods, the shape in shape relation of being raped by your gods would be more like the penitent entry of a lace barometer into your anus, than it would be like devastation.

How much of this would have to do with how much you really do in fact want it (from other planar lifetimes) whether or not your body in this planar lifetime has the wisdom or fortitude to recognize, then engage in it as submission and dominance relation, rather than rape?

Again, Marguerite Duras' writing—that you promised to take me to Marguerite Duras' grave.

To experience confoundment, but never abandonment—how this for my body would be a timeless key.

Perhaps this is at what exact situate Trans forms. Like getting your phantom limbs back through actions and engagements not exactly consensual, but surely requiring, filling and based in sacrifice. Scarification.

There are wisdoms that arise as slanted chivalries from these overlapped zones.

As the bloody bandages are removed, then wrapped back around the emanating site—pre blood is placed onto current blood—producing concurrent nectars.

j/j hastain

Consider this the larvae being marked—and somehow always also being swathed.

Consider this the cornucopia climaxing.

Tonal more than cognitive.

And then the carrions but so—renovation-ly.

Dear secondary umbilical,

It is sodden between my legs. I am both aroused and wretched—a sort of trembling, tumbling.

Pondering the devoted celibate being raped/ sodomized by their personal gods. This makes me dizzy—something like the way that for me sex and the constant potentials and potencies of the divine, can never be separated.

My first experiences of sex involved being bound at the wrists by an aggressive hand then pushed up against the great mahogany doors of the Mormon Church. Gods, edge and sex/ sensuality all intrinsically connected.

Also the consideration of what it would mean to be raped by a foreign body that would take me from behind and literally break me into hemolytic—the integral lyricisms that may be created there out of my moans—in order to articulate the experience of where agonies, struggles and redemptions that are diverse, non-cliché and admixed, admit themselves as beauty and erotic revolution.

This feels similar to a bit of food that is both savory and sweet at once—it feels somehow familiar to me, like literally taking in something that is not particularly palatable, but enjoying it all the way down.

Pondering this god that rapes.

Considering desiderate relations to.

j/j hastain

Dear secondary umbilical,

What all of this might mean for that body in the context of continuing to praise their gods. What all of this means for this body in the context of continuing to create these gods.

> Where do faith and event overlap?
>
> And from that overlap, what types of meaning will fuel a being to continue passed?

It is the most human hosanna to continue.

> Does sacrifice lead to contemporary periapt?
>
> Does the body sacrifice its balustrades or its personal understandings of ideology in order to expand?
>
> Who accounts for the body becoming more to itself, by somehow being forced to lose itself or temporarily discard itself?
>
> Where in the universe is this sort of information retained?
>
> In the context of cosmic truth, when if ever, does a being who has been raped by their gods get their un-raped anus back?
>
> Or do we spend the rest of our reincarnations experiencing phantom limb sensations in that tender area?

Dear secondary umbilical,

Will my orgasms intensify in other lives, related to what I have named the sanctimonies and violations that I had in my body in this life, because through those sanctimonies and violations my emotions and spirit were somehow made more gritty and authentic—more bare?

Has a portal or a wormhole to the anus been eternally made now?

The beads of the rosary bleed and sweat while passing through the cyborg's shaking hand.

Dear secondary umbilical,

Inter-planar loss has an effect on this planar body in form. This often occurs beyond languages or logics and definitely does not occur linearly.

The images are the only thing to ride there—the images and their sounds—like the soft rocking of wreckage. Like the sea slowly washing the pieces of the ship ashore—always both ravaged and lovely.

Superlative juice is being felt in the body as a frequency.

These are the golds that are gotten to through the reds.

If gods are not a linear construct and I am not a linear construct, these letters and visions are how I plan to make arduous and endless contacts with all that could intensify, alternate or add to divinity. Ever accumulating sanskrits, inventions and presses in order to be constantly producing a thing so deep and cosmically true, that it is in fact beyond agency.

Then the work from there, to experience that which exists beyond agency in form.

We looked down to see that the stilettos had been liquefied during the time that we were speaking.

at that site I remembered that females also know how to fuck primally
and a single apple protruded from the wormhole
a rapt periapt of spring

Dear secondary umbilical,

Water has been discovered in the polar regions of the moon. This matters because I have always believed that amrita[1] is literal.

Sacred fluid being secreted—the complicated, vast biologies that depend on just such fluid in order for creation to occur.

Because water is a polar molecule and has both positively and negatively charged ends, it has the aptitude to act as a universal solvent. It is an arc.

The merged parts said "if only to be like those frozen puddles—their reflections ever offering passage into the other worlds." Perhaps the regenerative cultivation of an endless liquid, in order to replace all lacerations and previous bouts of distress, is a suitable approach.

How the British prisoners (who as punishment were allowed to be given up to 800 lashings) after a time stopped feeling the pain—understood it as a dull hammering.

I wonder if the place that the body gets to in intensive environments and contacts such as this, is a liquid place.

    Can all liquid fuse with other liquid?

---

[1] that which is immortal—a nectar that is obtained through Guru's word--the place (believed to be geographically located in the moon) where deities and Devas store the liquid core of erotic power—the wetness within that correlates to the cave of Brahma in a human body

Is what we are ultimately awaiting as a species, the great reunion with ourselves as liquid seeped with and exuding liquid?

Through motion and smooth folding we are learning endless-reciprocal.

Oh supple mass.

Like baptism but baptism beyond permission to baptize.

Dear secondary umbilical,

> For the sake of pondering further, what would it mean to take the Jephthah's vow[1] inversely?
>
> To instill, strengthen or vivify whatever the next life that I come in contact with is?

Like chiseling into chrism. Like getting closer and closer to the it by way of lubricating the ducts via intuitions—through constructing rogue versions of door.

> For the sake of pondering further, what does it mean to make and then apply my own personal edens to time, space and relation?

Red ripe tomatoes to replace any gray that once existed in their place—like the onset of tears that are a fullness and are for fullness—oh sweet missives being bathed.

For things like this to be felt and sensed non-routinely; non-dually, I slowly eat the spindling.

Always waiting for you to come back and fuck me.

This complex work of cosmic oestrus—the palace that is woven out of both the intended ohms and the unexpected opera.

---

[1] those who take the Jephthah's vow, vow that as part of their holiness, they will kill the next being that they see

Dear secondary umbilical,

Always in order to consider yet another type of bondage.

> What effect would a shattered glass cock have on a sonorous fossa?—because a sonorous fossa is what my vagina, mouth and pores biomimic.

Something in the flickers, fracture and add to flexure like bits of candle wax collecting.

A mysterious meadow within, not to hurt me and never mundanely—this meadow within me in order to sustain fractally.

> What of the quantum is spasmodic access to things that have yet to be named?

There are granules that increase the elementals' abilities to rub in order to be refined—hallowed and without subtlety we come vigorously undone.

"This is my forever promise. To inseminate you with my urgencies."

How a question is an urgency is a culling or an extending of offing.

Dear secondary umbilical,

Unsure of whether or not I have a natural memory, I etch these pages as alchemical plumes because I identify curvature as deviant but not defiant. I am coming to define myself as inherently bowed—as succulent movements always inclusive of and being added to.

This is where segregations are averted, due to cling and closeness—oh fusions with the multi-chromatic.

How it is here in the applications and affiliations of the lumen-hymen that crisis becomes crystalline.

Yes, rain on a window—sonorous before visual.

All that this can do to ones previous precepts of negated.

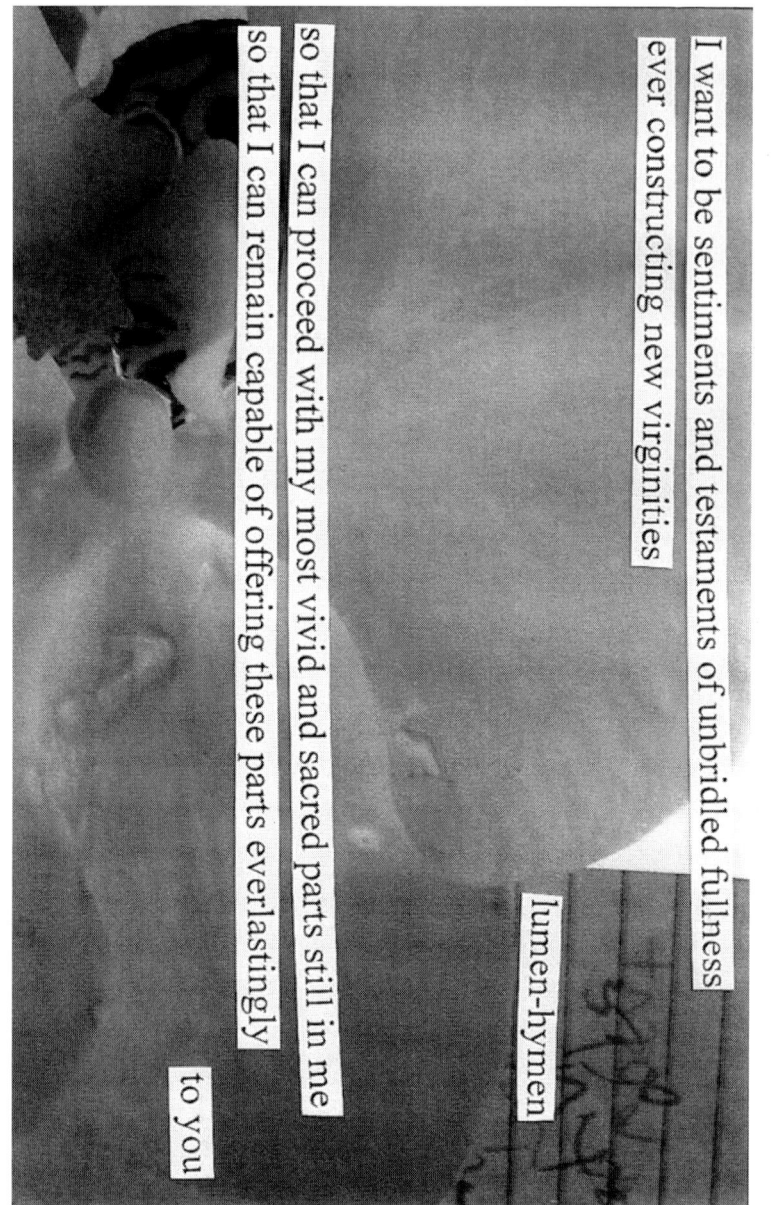

I want to be sentiments and testaments of unbridled fullness ever constructing new virginities so that I can proceed with my most vivid and sacred parts still in me so that I can remain capable of offering these parts everlastingly to you

lumen-hymen

Dear secondary umbilical,

The heart that waits for some deeper cosmic weight to release it into animateness. Oh benevolent-abyss.

"In Florence Italy there is a mass-based statue called Captives. It was near this statue that I felt vibrations as immanent. I knelt there and all I could do is release."

We trust the ulterior wombs as alternates to numbness.

We trust them because these wombs of ours are evolving us—peeling and shredding all facets of anti-activity, in order to enable us to refuse stasis.

Past stasis we pull at and fatten the elemental, sub-atomic hinges—we induce and perpetuate recitative.

Oh spasming, orbiculate hearth.

The collaborative work of other sides to the other side—where the options are not polar but are forever myriad.

Getting quieter now Dear secondary umbilical, as the questions and their relations combine.

Something like the complexity of an unending, non-euthanizable, fierce and relational, unrestricted masthead.

j/j hastain

Dear secondary umbilical,

As a lyrical anti-memoir, it is more important to me that I be retained (by eternity and the ether-spaces) as image, idea and composition—than it is that I be retained as any singular, completed, physiology or aesthetic.